Welcome to Salisbury Cathedral

M000087084

From whichever direction you approach Salisbury you will see the spire of Salisbury Cathedral, a beacon piercing the sky and drawing you near. There is so much that brings visitors to the Cathedral Church of the Blessed Virgin Mary (its official title), a remarkable and beautiful building with a fascinating history. Many come to see the finest of just four remaining originals of Magna Carta, to admire the magnificent medieval architecture, to search out other treasures within, to climb Britain's tallest church spire, or simply to picnic on the lawns of the Close. Others come as pilgrims, to join in as the choir lift their voices to Heaven at Choral Evensong, or to find a quiet corner for solace in prayer; for, very importantly, Salisbury Cathedral remains what it has always been – a place of Christian worship to which all are welcomed.

Front cover: **Salisbury Cathedral from the south-west.**

Old Sarum

Visitors to Salisbury are often surprised to learn that there was once an earlier cathedral, built on the summit of a chalk hill at Old Sarum (two miles north of today's cathedral) on what had been the site of an Iron Age settlement enclosed by an earth wall.

With a fortress and a location that was a meeting point of many Roman roads, Old Sarum became an important centre of communication, later added to by the Normans who built a castle here, the ruins of which can still be visited.

At the Council of London in 1075 it was decreed that bishoprics in villages should be moved to cities or

Above: Drawing of the City of Sarum. *Right:* Old Sarum, painted by John Constable (1776–1837).

IMPORTANT DATES

1000s	1100s	1200s	1300s	1400s
1075–91 First cathedral at Old Sarum built.	**1197** The Close, the site of today's cathedral, laid out.	**1215** Sealing of Magna Carta at Runnymede.	**1225** Dedication of three altars in the first part of the cathedral to be completed.	**1310–30** Tower and spire added.	**1445** Library built.
1092 Old Sarum consecrated; partially destroyed by fire but quickly repaired.		**1220** Foundation stones laid for the new Salisbury Cathedral.	**1258** Consecration of Salisbury Cathedral.	**1327** Wall built around the Close.	
				1386 Medieval Clock installed.	

towns; the dioceses of Sherborne and Ramsbury, held by Bishop Herman, were united into one new diocese at Old Sarum. Herman began building his cathedral here, and following his death in 1078, work continued under his successor, Bishop Osmund, who completed it in 1091. Just five days after the cathedral was consecrated in 1092, it was badly damaged by fire – most likely the result of being struck by lightning.

The undiscouraged Osmund repaired his cathedral, which was later extended by Bishop Roger and further still by Bishop Jocelin. The outline of the foundations of the cathedral at Old Sarum is still clearly visible.

1500s	1600s	1700s	1800s	1900s	2000s
1534–35 Henry VIII separates the Church of England from Rome during the Reformation.	**1640s** Salisbury Cathedral damaged during the English Civil War.	**1789–92** James Wyatt's restoration includes clearing the churchyard, demolishing the bell tower, lime-washing the vaulting, covering medieval paintings and removing much medieval glass.	**1862–78** Sir George Gilbert Scott's restoration includes adding new sculptures to the West Front and reproducing medieval paintings in the quire. **1876** 'Father' Willis organ installed.	**1980** Installation of Prisoners of Conscience window designed by Gabriel Loire.	**2008** Salisbury Cathedral celebrates 750 years with the installation of the William Pye font. **2015** Celebrations of 800th anniversary of the sealing of Magna Carta.

A New Cathedral

With its hilltop position, Old Sarum (its Iron Age name 'Searobyrg' meaning 'Fortress by a gentle river') was disadvantaged for several reasons: it was within the outer fortifications of the castle and there were regular disagreements between clergy and the military; there was insufficient housing for the canons in what had become a congested city; and the winds were so strong it was reported that 'the clerks can hardly hear one another sing'. The Dean of Old Sarum, Richard Poore, had long been planning a move for the cathedral.

It was a time when many towns were being created and the laying out of Salisbury was initiated by Dean Poore. The Close, situated on 80 acres belonging to Richard and his brother Herbert, Bishop of Salisbury 1194–1217, was the starting point of the new town and building commenced in 1197. Richard Poore, made Bishop in 1217 after his brother's death, was granted permission by the Pope to re-site the cathedral to a more favourable position. And so it was that in 1220 work began on a new cathedral at the centre of the Close and near to an all-important network of rivers which served the city of New Sarum.

The cathedral is built on a gravel terrace, the top of which is about 4 feet (1.2m) below ground level and is where the foundations start. Careful watch is kept on the water levels: the last serious flooding inside the cathedral – to ankle height – was in 1915, although in the 1630s flooding was apparently so great the clergy rode around on horseback.

Following the laying of the foundation stones on 28 April 1220 – an act performed by Bishop Richard Poore who, 'putting off his shoes, went in procession with the clergy of the church to the place of the

MASTER MASON AND ARCHITECT

Construction of the new Salisbury Cathedral was supervised by a mason, Master Nicholas of Ely, and the person most likely responsible for overseeing its Gothic architecture was a canon, Elias of Dereham. Amongst his other credits, Elias was titled 'The Most Honest Man in England' and given responsibility for circulating ten copies of Magna Carta, having been present at its sealing at Runnymede in 1215. A 1946 statue of him can be seen in the nave.

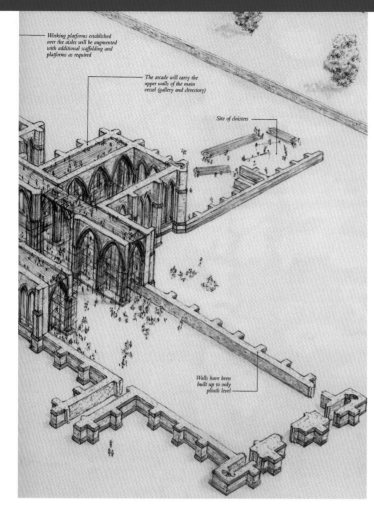

Working platforms established over the aisles will be augmented with additional scaffolding and platforms as required

The arcade will carry the upper walls of the main vessel (gallery and clerestory)

Site of cloisters

Walls have been built up to only plinth level

foundation singing the Litany' – work on the first section of the cathedral, the eastern end, progressed rapidly. Within five years the Trinity Chapel, flanked by the smaller St Stephen and St Peter Chapels, had been completed.

By 1258 work on the quire, transepts and nave was finished, and it is thanks to the speed with which the cathedral was built – a remarkable feat when one considers the basic equipment available to the craftsmen – that it remained in the English Gothic style for which the building is renowned. Maintaining its architectural integrity, it showcases the finest examples of three types of Gothic architecture: Early English, Decorated and Perpendicular.

Light, and its association with divinity, is an integral element of Gothic architecture. Originally, a lantern tower stood where the tower and spire now soar heavenwards. By the early 1240s all of its windows would have contained stained glass; as the 'eyes of the building' these would have flooded it with light.

Bishop Richard's vision was to build Salisbury Cathedral on a massive scale, with the likely purpose of rivalling Canterbury, Winchester and Lincoln Cathedrals. On its completion the interior of the cathedral measured 449 feet (135m) long and 84 feet (25.2m) at its highest point, exceptional in England at that time and only bettered 30 years later when Westminster Abbey's highest vaults reached just over 100 feet (30m) above ground. Three surviving additions have been made to the structure of Salisbury Cathedral since the 13th century: the tower and spire; strengthening arches at the crossings; and a small chantry chapel.

STICKS, STONES … AND ROYAL APPROVAL

The new cathedral was built from 60,000 tons of stone, much of it limestone quarried near Tisbury, 18 miles from Salisbury. Another limestone, Purbeck Marble, for columns, capitals and shafts came from the Isle of Purbeck in Dorset, gifted by Alice Brewer who owned a quarry at Dunshay. Although the source of the iron and bronze used remains a mystery, the 420 tons of lead were probably transported from the Mendip Hills. King Henry III donated some of the 2,800 tons of oak, to make roof timbers and doors, from his estates in Wiltshire and the recently conquered Ireland. So impressed was the King when he visited Salisbury in December 1225 that he later requested a similar basilica (double-aisled hall) be constructed at his new Temple Church in London.

Main image: Scissor arch in Salisbury Cathedral supporting the structure.
Left: Medieval stained glass.

The Trinity Chapel

Today, early morning Holy Communion is usually celebrated in the oldest part of Salisbury Cathedral: the Trinity Chapel, properly named the Chapel of Holy Trinity and All Saints. It is sometimes referred to as the Lady Chapel.

In 1226, the year after the Trinity Chapel was completed and consecrated, the bodies of three bishops of Old Sarum were re-interred here, including that of Bishop Osmund, whose coffin lid is displayed in the centre of the chapel.

The patterns of life established at the old cathedral were largely transferred to the new. Most cathedrals were then monastic but after 1066 nine English cathedrals, including Salisbury, adopted the secular format, meaning clergy were not all drawn from one religious order. From its earliest foundation the cathedral was ruled by a Chapter led by four Personae (the Dean, the Precentor, the Chancellor and the Treasurer); so successful was this method in managing the cathedral that it was embraced by many others in England and elsewhere.

In the early Middle Ages there was no universal model for Christian worship. The way great churches organised their affairs was known as their 'Use', and the Use of Sarum – initiated by Bishop Osmund and developed by Bishop Richard – came to have a unique influence in England. It did not follow a monastic pattern, and so reverent and dignified were the ceremonials that the Sarum Rite became the norm in most English churches. Even today it continues to influence the way Salisbury Cathedral and other great churches arrange their worship.

Above: Trinity Chapel. *Left:* The shrine of St Osmund. *Right:* The Prisoners of Conscience Window, made by Gabriel and Jacques Loire in Chartres, France.

The Trinity Chapel is dominated by its most striking feature: the Prisoners of Conscience Window, the most recent of a series of designs which have filled this space for centuries. When Sydney Evans was made Dean at Salisbury in 1977, he wanted to introduce more colour into the cathedral by providing a window reflecting a Christian response to worldwide violence and injustice. The result, unveiled in 1980, is the work of father-and-son team Gabriel and Jacques Loire. There is much to be seen as one studies the window: in the central lancet is Christ on the Cross, his head bowed; in the left and right lancets are the faces of both convinced and doubting prisoners.

Chantry & Other Chapels

Chantry chapels were built with funds donated to cathedrals by the rich. The expectation was that, following the donor's death, priests would chant masses for them, thus speeding their souls through Purgatory to the kingdom of Heaven. Chantry chapels were abolished by King Edward VI in 1547.

Despite the fact that in 1789 James Wyatt (the most fashionable architect of the day) was employed to remodel the cathedral and demolished two medieval chantry chapels at the east end – one for Bishop Beauchamp, the other for Lord Hungerford – Salisbury is fortunate to have retained the Audley Chapel. Built for Edmund Audley, Bishop 1502–24, this is an exquisite example of the Perpendicular style. The fan-vaulted ceiling still has some of its original colour and amongst the detail on the 'lattice' work is the emblem of Bishop Audley conjoined with a vandalised image of Mary (the Virgin); circling the whole are the linked emblems of King Henry VIII (red roses) and his first wife, Katherine of Aragon (pomegranates, representing fertility – and his expectations of her).

The original plan of the cathedral contained 13 chapels. Over the centuries their use and layout have changed. The Morning Chapel was originally two chapels, and was given its present name when used for the first service of each day. On the north wall is one of the cathedral's double aumbries, or safes, in which to keep consecrated bread, wine and oils. On the west wall is part of the 13th-century pulpitum (quire screen), which was removed during Wyatt's restoration (see pp.12–13).

Set into the pulpitum is a revolving, engraved glass prism by Laurence Whistler, dedicated to his artist brother, Rex Whistler, killed in action in Normandy in 1944.

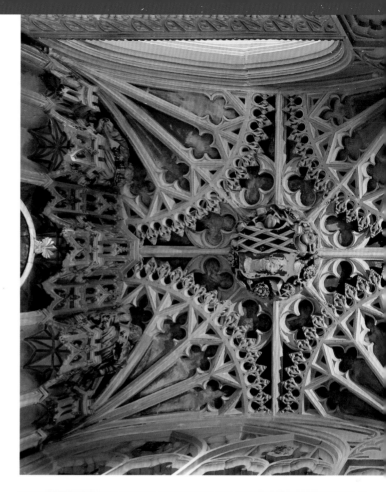

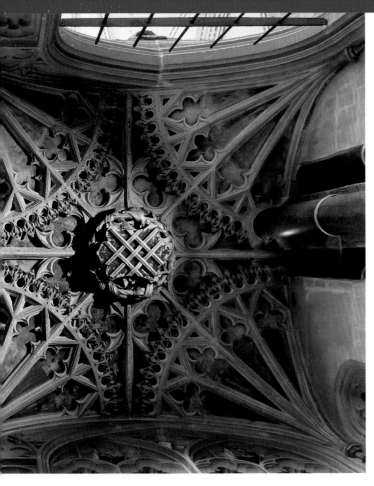

Above: The ceiling of the Audley Chapel.
Opposite, left: Inside the Audley Chapel.
Left: Whistler Prism (photograph by Peter Marsh). *Right:* The Morning Chapel.

AN INTRIGUING TOMBSTONE

Outside the Morning Chapel, in the floor of the north quire aisle, is the tomb of Thomas Lambert. Intriguingly his date of birth is given as 13 May 1683 and his date of death as 19 February 'the same year'. How could he have died three months before he was born? When the Julian Calendar was used in England, New Year's Day fell on 25 March – the Feast of the Annunciation, or Lady Day, so-called because it was nine months before Christmas Day and believed to be the day Christ was conceived; a subsequent move to the Gregorian Calendar saw the New Year starting on 1 January.

The Quire & Presbytery

The presbytery and quire is a 'church within a church', containing the focal High Altar and the place where Evensong is sung or said every day.

It was part of Wyatt's plan to open up the view down the length of the cathedral, and the medieval quire screen separating quire from nave was removed while the cathedral was closed during his 1789–92 restoration; part of this original stone screen can be seen in the Morning Chapel. The installation of a new organ, gifted by King George III, meant that in 1790 Wyatt had to replace the original screen with a larger one, big enough for the organ to sit on. This stone screen was replaced with an ironwork one in 1860. One hundred years later, however, the decision was made to remove the quire screen altogether, creating the dramatic vista enjoyed today.

There is much carving to be admired in the quire, including on the quire stalls – the largest complete set in Britain; the rear stalls on either side are the earliest, a gift from Henry III in 1236. The early 20th-century canopies over the rear stalls contain statues representing Bishops of Salisbury. Only one of the pre-Reformation bishops does not wear his mitre on his head: this is John Salcot (Bishop 1539–57), whose successful but hardly admirable career is perhaps why the carver represented him with his mitre at his feet.

The canopied Bishop's throne (or *kathedra*, the Greek word from which we get the word 'cathedral') is to the east of the quire stalls. Flanking the throne is a processional cross and croziers. The jewels in this magnificent silver cross came from a bracelet given by the wife of an Archdeacon of the cathedral whose son was killed in the First World War.

THOMAS BENNETT'S TOMB

In the north quire aisle is one of only two cadaver tombs in the cathedral: that of Thomas Bennett, Precentor of the cathedral who died in 1558. The canopy above his monument is inscribed 'A.D. 1554', suggesting it was prepared four years before his death. A shield on the tomb chest is marked 'Anno Domini 155_'; the final figure was never carved.

'FATHER' WILLIS ORGAN

Salisbury Cathedral's three organs provide a time-honoured accompaniment to its choirs. The principal instrument in the quire is the great 'Father' Willis organ, installed in 1877 as a generous bequest from Miss Chafyn Grove. Used almost daily in services, this organ, with almost 4,000 pipes, is regarded as one of the finest pipe organs in the country; in fact, Willis himself considered it his finest work.

The Tower & Spire

The spire of Salisbury Cathedral, soaring to 404 feet (123m), is the tallest and most glorious in Britain, renowned for its grace and delicacy, although it was not part of the original structure.

Standing outside the cathedral and looking up, keen-eyed visitors may spot the original crenellations of the 13th-century tower about 100 feet (30m) above ground level. In the early 14th century many cathedrals and abbeys in England were having something new added to make them bigger and grander, and around 1310–30, despite the shallow foundations at Salisbury Cathedral, two further stages were added to the square tower and topped by the magnificent octagonal spire.

And so the original lantern-tower roof was removed. The extra weight of the new tower and spire (around 6,500 tons) meant adjustments were vital, so flying buttresses were built internally and externally, and scissor arches were added in the quire transepts later in the 14th century. After a storm in 1360, oak scaffolding was installed inside the spire as reinforcement and still remains, as does a wooden windlass used by the builders to haul materials up; the hole for its rope is still visible in the 15th-century lierne-vaulted ceiling. The tower was also reinforced by complicated but elegant early 14th-century ironwork. The spire was a feat of engineering later admired by Sir Christopher Wren who considered it 'the finest of its kind in Europe'.

Despite these precautions, stress on the supporting walls caused the pillars to bend, and in the 15th century two great stone strainer arches were added at the central crossing. The tower and spire subsequently settled with a displacement of only 8 inches (20cm), though the bending of the pillars is clearly visible.

SAFE AS HOUSES

A survey by Sir Christopher Wren in 1668 detected the spire was leaning 29½ inches (75cm) south-west; the same degree of declination was noted in 1737 and a brass plate was inserted in the floor of the nave to mark the spot touched by a plumb line suspended from the top of the spire. Happily, no significant movement has been detected since.

Far right: The tower of Salisbury Cathedral. *Above:* Oak scaffolding inside the spire. *Right:* The windlass.

The Nave

Salisbury Cathedral's nave is a majestic space measuring 200 feet (60m) long and rising to 84 feet (25.2m) at its highest point. It is a great vantage point from which to view the three levels inside the cathedral: the aisles; the triforium (the arched gallery above the nave); and, highest of all, the clerestory, where windows allow light into the building.

Much of the glass in Salisbury Cathedral is plain; early stained glass was removed during the Reformation, and James Wyatt's restoration of 1789–92 saw other coloured glass removed. However, two grisaille windows containing much 13th-century glass can be seen at the west end of the nave aisles. In the 1860s, the cathedral's second major restoration period saw Sir George Gilbert Scott reversing a good deal of the earlier restoration, with new stained glass gradually replacing some of Wyatt's clear windows: two exquisite windows designed by Edward Burne-Jones and made by William Morris are in the south quire aisle.

A font is traditionally situated near the entrance of a house of God, representative of a beginning: that of being baptised at the start of the Christian journey. Salisbury Cathedral's font is a spectacular centrepiece to the nave and one of its modern treasures. The Living Water font, designed by British water sculptor William Pye, was installed on 28 September 2008, the eve of Michaelmas Day, as part of the 750th anniversary celebrations of the consecration of the cathedral which took place on Michaelmas Day in 1258. At a service presided over by the Archbishop of Canterbury, he consecrated the font and baptised two infants. The consecration mark of a

Vaulting in the nave.

William Longespée, 3rd Earl of Salisbury and half-brother to King John, had the honour of being the first person buried in Salisbury Cathedral. A great warrior, he led English raids in France in the early 13th century. Although it was said he died from poisoning (traces of arsenic were detected in a preserved rat found in his skull when his tomb was opened in 1719), it is more likely to have been from exposure to the elements after being shipwrecked, and his subsequent care (or lack of) by French nuns. He died at Old Sarum in 1226 shortly after his return to England; his tomb is in the nave.

The tomb of William Longespée.

cross made in oil by Archbishop Rowan Williams is still visible on all four sides of the green patinated bronze vessel. Water is a predominant feature: its still, smooth surface reflects the surrounding architecture; and an endless movement of water flows through spouts at the four corners before disappearing through a bronze grating in the floor. Words from Isaiah 43:1–2 that form part of the baptismal service are carved on the font, and include the line: 'When you pass through the waters, I will be with you.'

Another special treasure in the nave is the Medieval Clock. This hand-made iron instrument was made

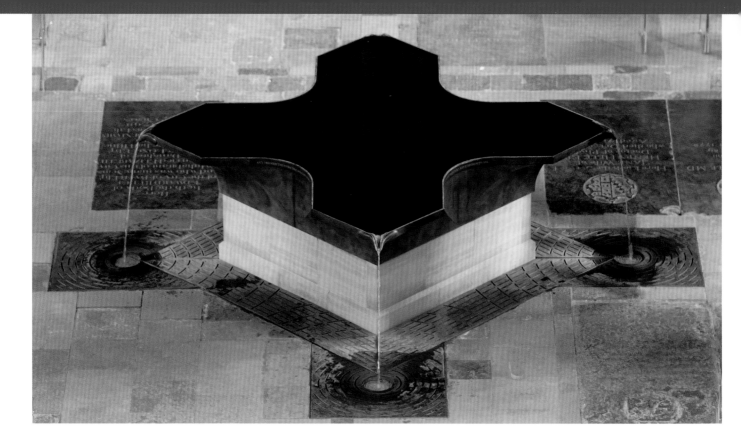

c.1386 and is likely to be the oldest working mechanical clock in existence. As is usual for the period, it has no face, being designed only to strike the hour. It was originally kept in the bell tower, which was separate from the cathedral. The bell tower was damaged during the English Civil War and was subsequently demolished by Wyatt, after which the clock was moved into the cathedral tower. It carried on working here until a new clock was installed in 1884, a gift from the Wiltshire Regiment which has a long association with Salisbury Cathedral and whose colours are displayed in the nave. The discarded Medieval Clock was rediscovered, no longer in working order, in 1929, but it was not until 1956 that it was repaired and restored.

Above: View of the font from the West Gallery.

Left: The Medieval Clock.

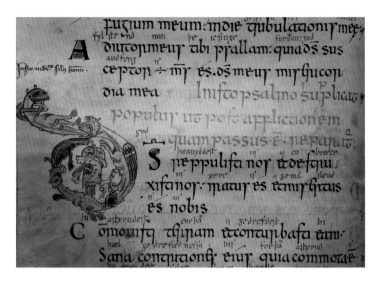

The Library & Archives

It was King Henry VI who encouraged the building of a library at Salisbury Cathedral. In 1445 a library and lecture room, reached by a spiral staircase and small stone bridge, were built over the eastern cloister. Originally twice the length it is today, the southern part of the library was taken down in 1758.

The library contains an ancient collection, which was started with many manuscripts written at Old Sarum and is continually being added to. Amongst the manuscripts is the library's earliest treasure: a page from the Old Testament written in Latin and dating from the 8th century. Among its many early printed books, there is a remarkable collection of early scientific, mathematic and medical works, bequeathed by Seth Ward (Bishop of Salisbury 1667–89) who had previously been Professor of Astronomy at Oxford and was a founder member of the Royal Society.

The treasury and muniment room, built to hold the cathedral's treasures and archive records, adjoin the south-east transept. This octagonal building is thought to have been added *c*.1250, the nature of its entrance suggesting it was an afterthought. In 1970 the large muniment chests were moved into the presbytery aisles, and the first-floor muniment room allocated for choir practice.

WREN'S NOTEBOOK

It was Bishop Seth Ward who asked his friend Sir Christopher Wren to survey Salisbury Cathedral, left in a sorry state after the Reformation and Civil War. Wren's notebook from August 1668 is preserved in the library, and records his view of this 'large and magnificent pile' and his suggestions for restoration.

Left, above: A 10th-century book of psalms in Salisbury Cathedral's library. *Left, below:* The library.

Magna Carta

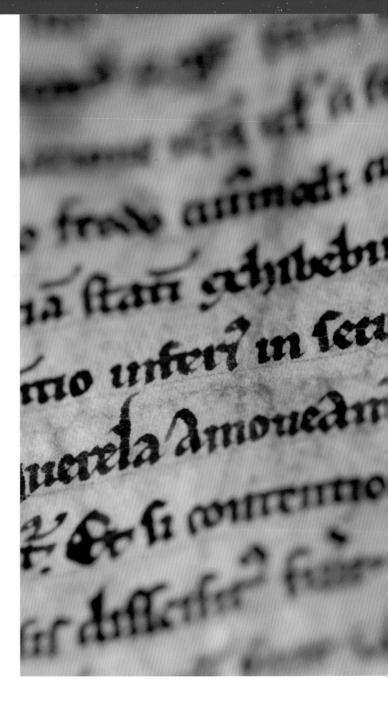

What draws many visitors to Salisbury Cathedral is its Magna Carta, one of only four surviving charters from 1215.

In 2015 the cathedral celebrates the 800th anniversary of the sealing of Magna Carta on 15 June 1215 at Runnymede, near Windsor. King John's 'Great Charter' was a bill of rights first drawn up by his rebellious barons and later refined by the Archbishop of Canterbury, Stephen Langton (*c.*1150–1228). Langton – along with others, including Elias of Dereham (his steward at that time and a keen negotiator) and the King's half-brother William Longespée – was present at the sealing and a key player in the crisis. It was probably Langton who was responsible for drawing up the barons' initial demands in a document known as The Articles of the Barons, now held in the British Library and from which Magna Carta was born.

Magna Carta was designed to regulate the feudal relationship between the King and his vassals, ensuring the Crown (and now the State) would act only by recognised legal procedures. The most famous of the 63 clauses states the fundamental principles of a fair trial: 'No free man shall be taken or imprisoned or deprived or outlawed or exiled or in any way ruined … except by the lawful judgment of his peers or by the law of the land.'

Magna Carta survived an initial annulment by the Pope, civil wars and various rewritings. The 1225 version, amended and reissued several times until 1297, still forms the basis of English law: three of the original 63 clauses still stand on the statute book. It was 575 years after its sealing that the personal liberties of the document guaranteed to Englishmen were incorporated in the USA's Bill of Rights.

Above: Salisbury Cathedral's Magna Carta. *Right, top:* Bronze statue of King John sealing Magna Carta. *Right, below:* The Magna Carta Exhibition.

Salisbury Cathedral's Magna Carta – in the best condition of the four that remain – was penned in 3,500 words of abbreviated Latin on sheepskin and is displayed in the Chapter House. The Charter even has an entry in the UNESCO 'Memory of the World Register'. A Magna Carta guidebook, which gives an extensive account of its history, is available in the cathedral shop.

The Chapter House & Cloisters

The Chapter House was a meeting place for the clergy of a cathedral. The governing body of a cathedral is still called a 'Chapter'.

Salisbury Cathedral's octagonal Chapter House was built in the mid-13th century, in a style similar to that at Westminster Abbey. Around the walls are stone benches where Chapter sat to discuss cathedral business. Above these is an intricate frieze depicting scenes from the first two books of the Bible; these were carved at a time when few people could read, allowing them to benefit from stories such as the Creation and the life of Joseph.

Carved heads on the arches are thought by some to be taken from life, reflecting a likeness of people present during the building of the Chapter House. One of them, facing the entrance, has three faces, possibly representing the Trinity. Following damage in the 17th century and years of neglect, the Chapter House, its carvings and most glass were skilfully restored in 1855–60. It was restored again in more recent years as part of the cathedral's major repair programme that began in 1985.

The entrance to the Chapter House is in the Cloisters, which were completed *c*.1266 and are the largest in England at 190 feet (58m) square. They were designed for processions, hence their width of 18 feet (5.5m), and as a place for reading and relaxation. The ceiling bosses are original and contain much intricate carving; some of the coloured paint which once decorated the Cloisters – and indeed much of the medieval cathedral – is still just visible.

Right: The eastern Cloister. *Above, centre:* The Cloister garth, with the two cedars of Lebanon. *Right, below:* The frieze in the Chapter House, scene depicting Noah's Ark.

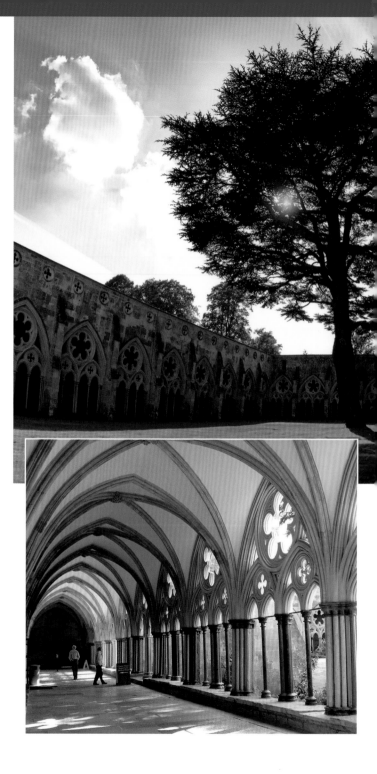

The Chapter House has a beautiful fan-vaulted ceiling that rises from a single column, which the author Daniel Defoe (who published an account of his travels through Wiltshire in the early 1720s) claimed moved when he leant on it!

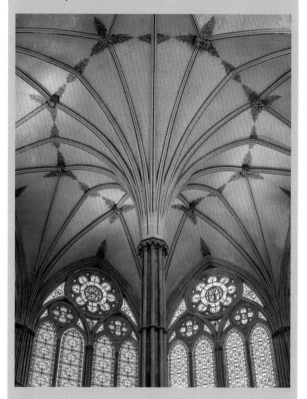

The Chapter House.

Central to the Cloisters is its garden, with two cedars of Lebanon planted in honour of Queen Victoria's accession in 1837. A more recent addition, unveiled in 2008 as part of the cathedral's 750th anniversary, is the sculpted head of the Angel Gabriel by artist Emily Young, who created it from the same Purbeck stone with which the cathedral is partly built.

The Cathedral Close

Arriving at Salisbury Cathedral through the archways of the North Gate or St Ann's Gate, visitors are struck immediately by a sense of calm as they enter the pretty green area that is the Close. This is the largest Cathedral Close in Britain, its stone houses for the medieval canons being constructed around the same time as the cathedral.

Although architect James Wyatt is often maligned for some of his restoration work at the cathedral, it was he who turned the Close from a muddy, swampy graveyard into the fine setting it is today, and a source of inspiration for writers and artists. Anthony Trollope conceived the plot for his first major success, *The Warden* (1855), after visiting Salisbury Cathedral; this was the first of his Barsetshire novels in which Salisbury becomes the fictional Barchester. William Golding taught English at Bishop Wordsworth's School here in the Close and one of his greatest works was *The Spire* (1964). *Sarum* (1987) by Edward Rutherford is a family saga set in Salisbury and nearby Stonehenge. The backdrop to Ken Follett's historic novel *The Pillars of the Earth* (1989) and its sequel *World Without End* (2007) is based on Salisbury, which in his books becomes the town of Kingsbridge.

Some of the houses in the Close retain traces of their 13th-century origins, though many were rebuilt after the Restoration in 1660 and became the homes of the rich and famous; others date from the early 18th century. Several of them have become visitor attractions. Arundells was the home of Edward Heath, England's Prime Minister 1970–74, and displays collections of his sailing, musical

Above, centre: **Arundells, the former home of Sir Edward Heath.**
Right: **Choristers Green.**

The Walking Madonna.

THE WALKING MADONNA

A particularly striking artwork in the Close is *The Walking Madonna*, a bronze created by Dame Elisabeth Frink in 1981. The position of this potentially life-size sculpture of Our Lady was chosen by Dean Sydney Evans; she strides from the cathedral into the wide world, where human needs are to be met.

and political memorabilia; he died in 2005 and his ashes are interred in Salisbury Cathedral. Mompesson House, a National Trust property, is a perfectly proportioned Queen Anne town house, with notable plasterwork and an elegant oak staircase. The Rifles (Berkshire & Wiltshire) Museum is housed in a Grade II listed building, where visitors can discover the story of the infantry regiments of the two counties. The award-winning Salisbury Museum contains archaeological collections of national importance, including several finds from Stonehenge and others connected with the Amesbury Archer, dating from around 2400 BC. Artworks include several by J.M.W. Turner, amongst them his *North Porch of Salisbury Cathedral*, painted c.1796.

A Musical Heritage

Music has been a central part of Christian worship from the earliest times, and Salisbury Cathedral has a great tradition of choral singing.

Old Sarum had a choir of boys and vicars choral, the latter deputised by singing services when the canons were unavailable. As early as 1091, Bishop Osmund founded a school for the choirboys and when the new cathedral was built they were taught in the Close. From 1714 the choir school was in Wren Hall where it remained for over 200 years, moving to the former Bishop's Palace in 1947. Now Salisbury Cathedral School is a thriving co-educational preparatory day and boarding school for 200 pupils aged 3–13, and teaches choristers in the cathedral's two world-famous choirs.

In 1991 Salisbury became the first English cathedral to give girls the same opportunities as their male

Centre: Salisbury Cathedral's choir in concert. *Below:* Children practise for the Cathedral School's jazz band.

BUMPING STONE

In the south quire aisle is the 'bumping stone', on which it is customary for any new member of the boys' choir to have his head bumped – but not so hard in modern times as in days gone by! Although there is an indentation in the stone, it is likely that this was created by a stonemason, rather than by numerous choirboys' heads. Girl choristers go through a different ritual: they are bumped on the head with a Prayer Book.

counterparts by forming a girls' choir. Along with the boys' choir, they help lead services, including daily Choral Evensong, plus concerts, tours and recordings. Many of these young people go on to pursue a musical career in adulthood.

Together with six lay vicars these choirs form the Cathedral's Choral Foundation. They are conducted by the Director of Music and are supported by an assistant organist and an organ scholar.

'Father' Willis organ.

A Living Cathedral

The cathedral's ambition in the 21st century is to make a difference for God through exceptional worship and outreach. Over 1,000 services take place here every year and everyone is welcome to these, including early morning worship with Holy Communion or Evensong, which happen daily, and any of several services held on Sundays. During the Sunday Eucharist the laying on of hands and anointing the sick with oil is available as part of the ministry.

The outreach programme sees the cathedral working at home and abroad to make a practical difference. Initiatives in the wider world include further developing close links with the Church of Sudan and South Sudan, and supporting disaster appeals. Closer to home, the cathedral contributes by volunteering in the local community, leading projects for specific groups (everything from stone carving for schoolchildren to art and literacy projects for community groups), offering resources at local and regional events, and engaging in charitable activity.

Young people are the lifeblood and future of the cathedral, which works to support the development of Salisbury Cathedral School, not only a training ground for cathedral choristers but one where spiritual enrichment is paramount. Visiting schools on educational trips, other groups and individuals are always warmly welcomed by dedicated volunteers who are proud to enhance the curriculum and show what the cathedral has to offer.

Ancient and modern artworks are an important part of life at the cathedral. Some are permanent and can be enjoyed time and again; others form part of changing exhibitions, regularly offering new delights for visitors.

DARKNESS TO LIGHT

Special services take place at specific points throughout the year. One of these is the spectacular *Darkness to Light* which marks the beginning of Advent. Starting in total darkness and silence, a programme of music, readings and prayer follows, as processions throughout the building culminate in the cathedral being lit by over 1,300 candles.

Left: Darkness to Light service. *Above:* The Night Visions event at Salisbury Cathedral. *Right, top:* The Nicholas Pope Exhibition, May 2014. *Right, below:* An altar frontal.

Of particular note is the work of the embroiderers, whose remarkable and imaginative needlework adorns altar frontals and hassocks throughout the cathedral, as well as robes of the clergy, including the skilfully worked processional copes used on feast days. Traditionally these would have been stored in the enormous *c.*13th-century oak cope chest now in the south nave aisle.

Perhaps most significant of all is the fact that this house of God continues to be what it has always been – a living cathedral: a place of change, energy and calm; a place of Christian worship and beauty; a place for everyone.

Restoration & Conservation

For centuries, working to restore and maintain the splendour of Salisbury Cathedral has been part of its heritage, from the time of the Reformation and English Civil War, when part of the building was damaged, to the present day.

Even in the late 17th century the cathedral was a revered feature in the national landscape, and James Wyatt's controversial restoration in the 18th century sparked a movement towards more sympathetic conservation work to Britain's historic monuments. By the mid-19th century Wyatt's alterations seemed dated, and when Sir George Gilbert Scott started his restoration programme in the 1860s, he reversed much of Wyatt's work.

Although the exterior of the cathedral has changed little since Wyatt's time, a significant part of Scott's plan saw new statues added to the medieval West Front and, later that century, the North Porch was restored by Scott's successor, George Edward Street. However, by the end of the 19th century the cathedral's prosperity was waning; historic endowments were removed by Parliament and no future Bishop or Chapter were wealthy enough to fund the great building works that had gone before.

For several decades only low-level maintenance work was carried out and by the 1960s the need for more significant repairs was realised. In 1985 a major restoration appeal by the Cathedral Trust commenced, under the patronage of HRH Prince Charles. Since that time work has been completed on the spire and tower, the West Front, the roofs and the north side.

The major repair work will be completed by 2018 and has involved a range of craftsmen and women including